The Prestige Series

Crosville

Atkins

Transport Archive

D1465015

© 2001 J M Banks & G H F Atkins
ISBN 1 898432 39 2

Front cover: An evocation of the classic portrait of a green Tilling fleet in the 1950s. Fleet number **SLG147** (**LFM 728**), a 1950 Bristol L5G with standard Eastern Coach Works 35-seat bodywork, served after withdrawal by Crosville in the Cheshire Constabulary as a mobile road safety exhibition. It was later acquired for preservation, from 1982 under the aegis of the Company. *(John Robinson)*

Back cover: Crosville issued a series of very useful handbooks which gave details of routes, vehicles and depots. This was 1950's edition, at two shillings and sixpence (or a half-crown - 12$^1/_2$ pence, not allowing for inflation) rather expensive then for a young bus spotter but well worth saving up for. *(STA)*

Title page: A dramatic view of the Menai Bridge in August 1959 with Crosville's 1956 Bristol LD6B Lodekka fleet number **DLB851** (**808 AFM**) on its way into Bangor. *(GHFA)*

Below: The coaches outside Crosville's garage at Mostyn Broadway, Llandudno, in July 1970 were still in Crosville's cream livery although this was eighteen months into the National Bus Company's existence. The vehicles are **CVF694** (**XFM 694G**), a 1969 Duple-bodied Bedford VAM70; **CMG358** (**806 FFM**), an Eastern Coach Works bodied Bristol MW6G of 1958; and **CMG482** (**2188 FM**), a similar machine dating from 1963. *(GHFA)*

>> *Opposite page:* A Crosville Leyland Lion passes beneath the Eastgate Clock in Chester. The vehicle, No. **200** (**FM 4334**), was a 1927 PLSC3 with Leyland 35-seat bodywork, which lasted in service with the Company until 1949. The lack of provision for a destination box was in accordance with Crosville's policy of using WID boards, usually in the lower saloon front bulkhead window. "WID" was the trade mark of the company which manufactured these information boards (NB - none is in use on this Lion, but see later in the book where several examples are illustrated on a variety of vehicles). *(STA)*

CROSVILLE

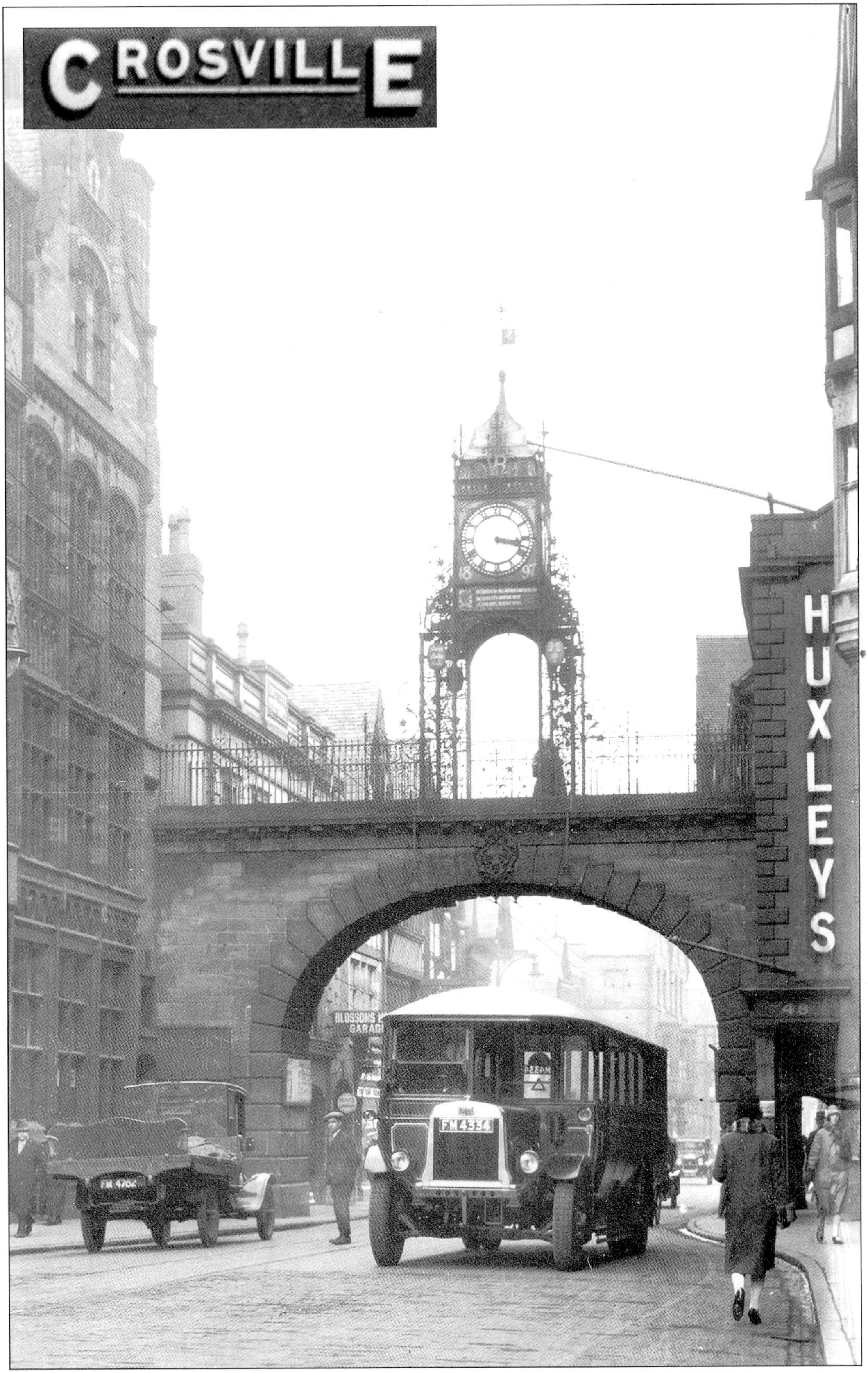

INTRODUCTION

Crosville Motor Services Limited was in some ways a sickly child and might well not have survived at all, let alone become one of the biggest of the companies which would, in 1942, form part of the Tilling Group.

For a start, it was never intended that it should be a bus company. Crosville originated in the first decade of the 20th Century in a none-too-successful agreement to manufacture and market motor cars to the design of a Frenchman, Georges Ville. The man making the agreement was George Crosland Taylor, a Yorkshireman. The first syllable of his second given name plus Ville's surname produced one of the most familiar words in the British passenger transport industry.

In 1906 premises at Crane Wharf, Chester, were acquired for motorcar production by a newly formed company, the Crosville Motor Company Limited. It seems that work was not started on building the first Crosville car until 1908 and only five ever took to the road.

The fledgling enterprise was clearly going to make nobody rich and, in 1910, it was decided to diversify into motor passenger transport on a route between Chester and Ellesmere Port: a journey that could not be made direct by train. This began operation in 1911 and early chassis used to try to keep it running were of Herald, Germaine and Albion manufacture.

These early years were beset by alarming financial losses, a situation not reversed until April 1913. In that year a modest profit was made and the services operated were Chester to Ellesmere Port, Chester to Kelsall, and Nantwich to Crewe and Sandbach.

The difficult financial straits in which the Company found itself in those first years left an indelible mark. Economies were ever afterwards constantly sought, even to the extent of substituting lower wattage light bulbs and letting windows into roofs in order to dispense with the need for artificial lighting. Cost-consciousness was also evident in the one penny Bell Punch ticket. Other values could be for either a single or return journey. The penny ticket could be used only as a single, and so was printed half size.

The First World War put a stop to any thought of expansion to Crosville's small portfolio of routes, but much work was obtained conveying workers to and from the Queensferry munitions factory. Claude Crosland Taylor, George's second son, was now involved, and had been since April 1911, and the fleet began to expand.

Expansion was therefore tentative until the war was over, although the first acquired operator - Lightfoot, of Kelsall - had come as early as 1911, but thereafter was rapid; by 1926 Crosville's territory stretched from Liverpool to Cardigan and from Crewe to Caernarvon.

Purchases of new vehicles in the immediate postwar period were generally from Daimler and AEC. In order to prevent smaller operators from succeeding, Crosville also invested in some small ex-RFC Crossley tenders. The Company openly referred to the latter as "chasers", thus leaving no doubt as to their deliberate harrassing and forcing out of business other men whose living was drawn from the passenger transport industry.

Other makes acquired, mainly via the acquisition of competing businesses, in the early period included Albion, Bristol, Chevrolet, Dennis, Dodge, Fiat, Ford, GMC, Guy, Karrier, Lacre, Pagefield, SOS, Straker Squire, Tilling-Stevens and Vulcan.

In 1921 the first Leyland arrived; from then until 1940 the Lancashire manufacturer supplied most of Crosville's new chassis.

It is often assumed that the involvement of the Big Four railway companies in bus operation was a simple business decision, achieved by mutual agreements. This was far from the case. The Railway Road Powers Bill had not survived its passage through Parliament in 1924. They bided their time and tried again, and on 3rd August 1928 were successful. The railway companies had been put under much pressure by bus competition in the 1920s: they had the financial strength to hit back, and now they had the legal authority as well. W J

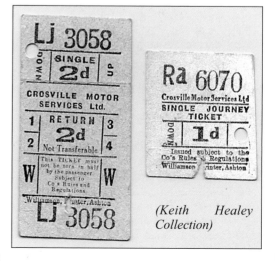

(Keith Healey Collection)

4

Crosville's greatest competitor in North Wales in the 1920s was Brookes Brothers, of Rhyl, whose flamboyant white-painted vehicles ran under the fleetname "White Rose". If White Rose gave Crosville trouble on the road as a competitor (which it undoubtedly did), that was nothing to the difficulties involved when, in 1929/30, Crosville (by then owned by the LMS Railway) attempted to buy, and eventually succeeded in buying, the White Rose business. The fleet of over 80 vehicles included a majority of Leylands, some of which served their new owner into the 1950s. This 1925 SG9, with Leyland dual-doorway bodywork, was White Rose No. 51 (DM 4115). It became Crosville's No. 454 but had gone by 1932. (STA/BCVM)

Crosland Taylor, in *"The Sowing and the Harvest"*, put it succinctly: *"It looked as if in 1928 we should ... certainly get stung. During the first months of the year we held on hard, but the tide was running strongly against us and I think all operators must have known in their hearts that the end was near, and there would have to be a showdown."* In 1929 the Company sold out to the LMS.

The Crosville name remained, though. So did Claude and W J, as employees of the LMS. W J opined that there was value in a name: *"It costs nothing, but people swarm round it like bees round their queen."*

The period of LMS direct rule was not a happy one; it lasted just a year. On 1st May 1930 a new company, Crosville Motor Services Limited was formed. Half the shares were owned by the LMS and half by Tilling & British Automobile Traction.

Claude Crosland Taylor died in 1935 and was succeeded as Managing Director by his brother W J Crosland Taylor. On 10th December 1942, in midwinter and at the black and grim height of the Second World War, W J dictated an inter-departmental minute to his Heads of Departments, Divisional Superintendents and Depot Superintendents, recording that a week earlier, on 3rd December 1942, the Company

had come under the direct control of Tilling Motor Services Limited. Among other things, he wrote, this meant *"that instead of getting help in various matters from the B.E.F. we shall in future get it from what is known as the Tilling Association Ltd."*

What he did not say at that stage was that the change in administration would see the end of the maroon livery and the entry into the fleet of Bristol and Eastern Coach Works products. The latter in their Tilling green livery would emerge in some strength in the postwar years until, on 1st January 1969, Crosville became part of the National Bus Company. The many changes since then are not within the remit of this book which attempts to record what to enthusiasts of a certain age is the "real" Crosville.

The bulk of the photographs used in this album were taken by G H F Atkins; publisher and author must once again record their thanks to Geoffrey for so willingly and helpfully making his work available for yet another *Prestige Series* volume.

Readers who have read earlier volumes in this series will be familiar with the GHFA method, particularly from the earlier years when photography was a more expensive hobby than it is today. Every exposure from the old eight-on-a-roll films had to count. To this end, an

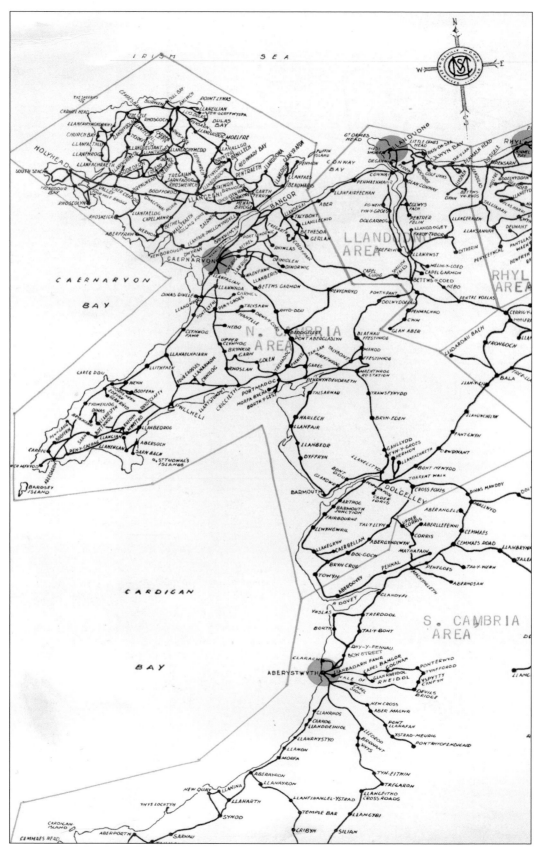

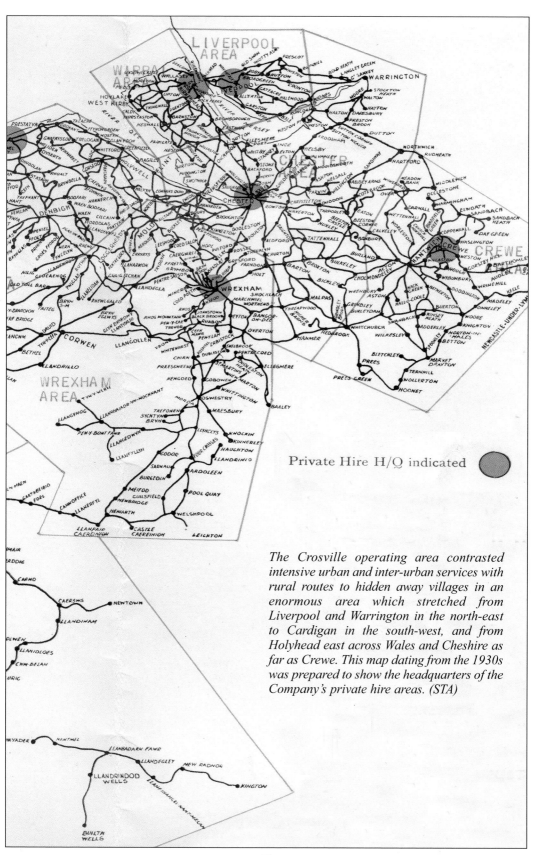

Private Hire H/Q indicated

The Crosville operating area contrasted intensive urban and inter-urban services with rural routes to hidden away villages in an enormous area which stretched from Liverpool and Warrington in the north-east to Cardigan in the south-west, and from Holyhead east across Wales and Cheshire as far as Crewe. This map dating from the 1930s was prepared to show the headquarters of the Company's private hire areas. (STA)

The Crosville "express saloon coach services" between Liverpool and surrounding towns to London became as celebrated as United's Tyne-Tees-Thames runs and at various times the two operators had similar vehicles serving the Capital. These leaflets of 1933 and 1953 illustrate Leyland Tiger and Bristol L coaches. The 1933 leaflet claimed that the London services were "service routes providing the interest of a coach tour through the historic heart of England." (Keith Healey Collection)

uncanny skill was built up and a fine collection of bodywork portraits amassed. Much of Geoffrey Atkins's photography was done during his annual holidays: he holidayed often in North Wales where many Crosville types were seen and photographed. Where Geoffrey missed recording certain types, particularly the early ones, the riches of the Senior Transport Archive and the Cull Collection have filled the gaps.

Others have helped, too, and without that help this book would have been much the poorer: John Senior opened his remarkable photographic and documentary archive, as well as reading the proofs and suggesting a number of improvements to the text; the British Commercial Vehicle Museum *(BCVM)* at Leyland courteously gave permission for the reproduction of Senior Transport Archive *(STA)* material originating many years ago from the old Leyland Motors Limited; Ron Maybray, as always, willingly supplied details of early vehicles from his immaculate written records; Arnold Richardson drew the writer's attention to the splendid Omnibus Society (Midland Branch) Cull Collection of photographs and kindly supplied prints; Keith Healey provided items of Crosville ephemera; David and Mary Shaw have once again read the proofs. Grateful thanks to all.

The PSV Circle fleet histories of Crosville and the books *"Crosville Motor Services - The First 40 Years"* by John Carroll and Duncan Roberts, published in 1995 by Venture Publications Limited, and *"75 Years of Crosville"* by John Carroll, published in 1981 by the Transport Publishing Company Limited, were valuable aids to caption-writing and are essential reading for those wishing to know the full story of Crosville's early vehicles. Worthy of special mention is the celebrated book *"The Sowing and the Harvest"*, by W J Crosland Taylor, in a new edition published in 1987 by the Transport Publishing Company Limited.

John Banks
Romiley, Cheshire
May 2001

CROSVILLE ON SOLID TYRES

Above: Crosville became a Leyland customer in 1921 and over the next 20 years purchased more than 1,300 chassis. The earliest were based on the GH7 model with 36hp engines and Leyland 32-seat bodywork. This pair, Nos **63/4** were photographed when brand new. They would be registered **FM 2173/4** and were part of a batch of twelve 36hp machines delivered in 1922. They were fitted with electric headlamps and acetylene sidelamps. The figure alongside No. 63 is believed to be Wally Wright, the Chief Engineer. *(STA/BCVM)*

Below: Early *chars-à-bancs* often had a rather fearsome appearance. In fact they were very comfortable and ran smoothly and silently with their petrol engines and solid rubber tyres (or *bandages* as the French would say). The comfort aspect was somewhat compromised when it rained, but on a glorious sunny day with the hood down a gentle run to the seaside was to be relished. Crosville's No. **12** (**FM 2848**) was a 1924 Leyland GH7LW with 32 seats. This is the period of the grey livery: Crosville were known as "The Greys". *(STA/BCVM)*

CROSVILLE ON SOLID TYRES

Above: There was always a need for small buses. Somehow, yesterday's small-scale "proper" buses seemed more appropriate for the job than the converted light goods vans seen in more recent times. Number **85** (**FM 2458**), a 20-seater, was based on the Leyland A7 chassis with 30hp engine; it had Leyland bodywork and was new in 1923. *(STA/BCVM)*

Below: Number **82** was another 1922 delivery. The GH7LW chassis was modified to semi-forward control specification, allowing the Leyland-built bodywork to seat 40. It was one of a pair, which were the only 1922 vehicles to survive in Crosville ownership into the thirties. They were withdrawn in 1931. This style of body, divided internally into two compartments, was called "The Crosville" by Leyland, although it had originally been built for Brookes Brothers. Dual lighting is again in evidence. *(STA/BCVM)*.

PNEUMATIC TYRES

Above: The trials and tribulations of the early history of the pneumatic tyre for use on heavy vehicles were eventually overcome. Use of pneumatics was one of the more important developments during the 1920s and Crosville was not slow to adopt them: this Leyland C7R arrived in 1925. One of three, No. **164** (**FM 3220**) had a Leyland 32-seat body and lasted until 1932. Note the rear ladder for access to the luggage rack. *(STA/BCVM)*

Below: By 1927 private hire passengers were rolling along on pneumatic tyres with side windows to keep the rain out. Number **268** (**FM 4304**) was one of a batch of six Leyland PLSC1 Lions with 32-seat all-weather coachwork by Queens Park. The hood could be closed or open, the windows up or down, or any combination of the two. It was rebodied by Eastern Counties as a service bus in 1933 and ran thus until 1938. *(STA/BCVM)*

TILLING-STEVENS

Above: The characterful Tilling-Stevens was one of many popular chassis which lost sales under the combined onslaught of Leyland and AEC products in the 1930s. Crosville's No. **867** (**UN 4488**), a 1931 B10A2, was acquired with the fleet and business of the Western Transport Company Limited, of Wrexham, on 1st May 1933. It is seen in June of that year at Llandudno, still in Western livery but carrying its Crosville fleet number. The 32-seat bodywork was by Brush, of Loughborough. *(GHFA)*

Below: What would later be number 880 in the Crosville fleet, (**FM 7058**), a similar machine, is seen when brand new in 1932. Whereas No. 867 was withdrawn in 1938, this one ran for Crosville until 1949. Both are examples of the BEF standard single-decker of the period. *(STA)*

CROSVILLE IN THE LANDSCAPE

Above: By the early 1930s Crosville's territory was well-established and its buses were part of the scenery. In June 1933, Geoffrey Atkins took a picture of the Conway suspension bridge when Crosville's No. **534** (**CC 8562**) happened to be crossing. The vehicle was a 1929 Ransomes-bodied SOS acquired in 1931 from the Llandudno Coaching and Carriage Company Limited, which had traded as "Royal Blue". Crosville and other road users pressed for decades for this bottleneck to be eliminated but it would be many years before the new bridge, alongside the old, relieved the problem. *(GHFA)*

Below: A group of men, perhaps going to church (or were they heading for the pub?) spare not a glance for No. **202** (**FM 3773**), a 1926 PLSC1 Lion, as it meanders through the streets of Chester. The vehicle was a 32-seater, bodied by Leyland. It was photographed soon after delivery. *(STA)*

Brand new number **271** (**FM 4486**), a 1927 PLSC3 "long Lion", as Leyland unofficially called them, also had the fine architecture of Chester as a setting. This 35-seater was rebodied in 1936 by Eastern Counties and withdrawn in 1949. The wires and the tram tracks confirm that the city's ancient trams were still operating. They were replaced by new AEC buses after the successful passage through Parliament of the Chester Corporation Act, 1929. *(STA)*

The Leyland Lioness 6 was a luxurious petrol-engined vehicle, clearly a close relation to the largest, most comfortable contemporary private cars, which was often, but by no means always, bought for private hire work. Crosville's No. **17 (FM 5247)**, seen here when new in May 1929, was a 24-seater with canvas roll-back roof bodied by United Automobile Services Limited, of Lowestoft. The livery was now green and grey. FM 5247 was withdrawn by Crosville in 1936. *(STA/BCVM)*

REBODIED LIONS

Above: Bodywork built in the 1920s was often outlived by the chassis carrying it and there were many rebodying programmes. Crosville was unusual, however, in basing a substantial programme on the PLSC Lion chassis. **DM 5260**, a 1927 PLSC3 acquired from White Rose Motor Services in 1930, was built with Leyland 36-seat bodywork and became Crosville's fleet number 424. It was rebodied by Eastern Counties (formerly United Autombile Services) at Lowestoft and in Crosville's 1935 renumbering scheme became **B90**. Similarly rebodied No. **B37** (**FM 5241**), a 1929 Lion which had been new to Crosville in 1929, stands behind. The livery had changed to LMS maroon. *(STA)*

Below: Number **78** (**FR 8419**) came from W Webster, who traded as UNU Motors, of Caernarvon, in 1930. A PLSC3 front-entrance 35-seater dating from 1928, it was rebodied by Eastern Counties for Crosville as a rear-entrance 35-seater. It was withdrawn in 1938. The oval transfer should be noted; for a brief period the same design carried LMS lettering and the railway coat of arms appeared on the back of the vehicles. Note also the classic WID plate in the bulkhead window, in lieu of a traditional roller-blind indicator, for which there was in any event no provision. *(GHFA)*

THE TITAN REVOLUTION

It could be thought ironic that the railway companies became so heavily involved in bus operation from 1929, for they inherited a major problem of their own making in the shape of hundreds of bridges, carrying their tracks over roads, that would not permit the passage of covered-top double-deck buses. The great G J Rackham, during his brief tenure at Leyland Motors, designed the Titan, which successfully combined a higher seating capacity than in contemporary single-deckers, the covered top that was then essential for passenger comfort if they were to be attracted to bus travel, and a low enough overall height to enable passage beneath railway bridges. Crosville's No. **645 (FM 6916)** was a TD2 model, with Leyland 51-seat "lowbridge" bodywork, which was long-lived in the fleet, not being withdrawn until 1954. These photographs, taken on 31st October 1931 when the bus was brand new, show the magnificent maroon livery and the oval logo that combined fleetname and number. *(Both: STA/BCVM)*

THE LEYLAND TITAN

Above: Earlier examples of the Titan were TD1s, the first of which had open staircases and platforms. Number **328** (**FM 5209**), another Leyland-bodied 51-seater, was a 1929 addition to the fleet. The earlier method of displaying the fleet number and the Company's name is shown. It is just possible to see that the upper-deck seating is of the four-in-a-row type. The livery here is the red that succeeded the grey and enjoyed a brief vogue before the maroon. *(STA)*

Below: A view, taken at West Shore, Llandudno in June 1933, which shows how Crosville advertised itself in the front destination screen. The places served by the bus appeared on WID boards in the upper- and lower-deck front nearside windows and adjacent to the platform. The bus was No. **794** (**FM 7763**), a TD2 that had been new the previous month. *(GHFA)*

This view of the Promenade at Rhyl in the 1930s happened to include Crosville's No. **219 (FM 6272)**. In another variation on the 51-seat Titan with Leyland bodywork theme, this was a TD1 (of 1930) with enclosed staircase and platform. The vehicle ran on producer gas during the war and survived into the postwar period. *(STA)*

The Titan's single-deck equivalent was the Tiger. This 1929 example, No. **177** (**FM 5224**), was a TS2 bodied by Leyland as a 25-seat dual-doorway coach. It was in Oxford Road, Llandudno, in June 1933. Rebodied by Eastern Coach Works in 1936/7, it lasted into the 1950s. (*GHFA*)

The next fleet number, No. **178 (FM 5225)**, is seen after conversion to a 32-seater and repaint into service-bus livery. It was - as was No. 177 - working the Liverpool to North Wales and Anglesey express service, and was also in Oxford Road, Llandudno in June 1933. *(GHFA)*

LEYLAND LIONS AND TIGERS

Above: In another June 1933 Llandudno shot, No. **467** (**FM 6430**), a 1931 Leyland Lion LT2 with Leyland 35-seat bodywork, was in Vaughan Street. *(GHFA)*

Below: The North Wales coastal resorts brought in traffic from a wide area. Number **614** (**FM 6452**) had arrived in Llandudno on the Potteries - North Wales Express from Newcastle-under-Lyme. The photograph is another taken in Oxford Road, Llandudno, in June 1933. The vehicle was a 1931 TS2 Tiger with dual-doorway 25-seat bodywork by Leyland. The superb paintwork on all these vehicles is worthy of note. *(GHFA)*

LEYLAND LIONS AND TIGERS

Above: Close-up detail of the bonnet, entrance and step arrangements of Leyland-bodied LT3 Lion 32-seater No. **558** (**FM 6908**) at Llandudno in the summer of 1933. The plethora of safety exhortations to passengers included the usual "Passengers off the bus first please" and "Wait until the bus stops" as well as one on the door into the saloon advising passengers not to cross the road behind the bus (or "car" as Crosville had it) until the road was clear. *(GHFA)*

Below: Two intrepid lady holidaymakers, carrying suitcases and unsuitably clad in heavy black overcoats and hats despite the blazing June 1933 sunshine, alight from No. **744** (**FM 7471**) in Caernarvon. The 32-seat Tiger TS4 coach had arrived from Merseyside and had travelled express via Abergele, Llandudno and Bangor. The coaching livery carried by No. 744 was a most attractive green and grey. This vehicle was one of several described officially by Crosville as "not coaches, but buses de luxe for express services". Roller blind indicators have finally arrived, to the relief, no doubt, of those who had to change the former route boards. *(GHFA)*

THE LEYLAND CUB

Leyland's Cub, built in their Kingston, Surrey, factory, was perhaps as important a step forward in the small bus category as had been the Titan and Tiger for larger vehicles. A harmonious design, largely based on contemporary large private car practice, it took business away from many other - mainly foreign - chassis makers. Crosville's No. **704** (**FM 7431**) entered service in 1932 fitted with 20-seat bodywork by Brush, of Loughborough. The destination screen again carries Crosville's fleetname. The use of route boards in the front window gave rise to Ministry criticism: it was alleged that the driver's vision was adversely affected, and smaller boards had to be provided. *(Both: STA)*

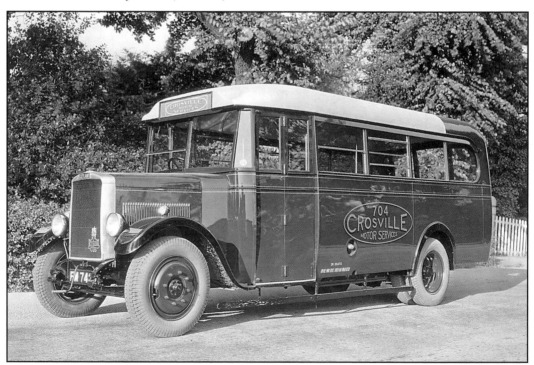

THE 1935 RENUMBERING

The original, simple numerical sequence used for Crosville fleet numbers had lost a lot of its orderliness by the mid 1930s. Acquired vehicles and new stock were rather haphazardly numbered and the prime purpose of fleet numbers - to easily identify the type and use of the vehicle - was lost. In 1935 a new system was started in which each type, and sometimes sub-type, had its own letter with each lettered series starting from 1. Thus, for example, normal control Leyland Cubs became the N class, represented *(above)* by **N27** (**FM 7437**), which formerly had been No. 710. Leyland Tigers went into the K class, and in the picture below **K81** (**FM 8166**), a 1934 Harrington-bodied front-entrance 33-seat Tiger TS6, which had been fleet number 933, is seen at the head of a convoy of private hire vehicles for the 4th Battalion Royal Welch Fusiliers. Following was **R47** (**FM 7057**), another of the ex-Western Transport Tilling-Stevens B10A2s acquired in 1933, which had been allocated the number 879 when taken over. *(Omnibus Society Midland Branch/Cull Collection; STA)*

This scene in Liverpool is taken from part of a negative exposed for the city's riverside architecture, including the Liver Building. Not primarily intended as a bus photograph, it nevertheless has a group of Crosville Leylands, led by an enclosed-staircase TD1 Titan, by then - as this is an August 1937 photograph - in the L class. *(GHFA)*

K-CLASS LEYLAND TIGERS

Above: **FM 7468** was originally No. 741. A 1933 Leyland-bodied Tiger TS4 coach with 32 seats, it was renumbered **K68** in the 1935 scheme. It was fitted with an oil engine in 1939 and renumbered as a KA vehicle *(see below)*. It lasted with Crosville until 1958.

Below: Harrington-bodied Leyland TS6 Tiger **FM 8165** had the identity 932 when new in 1934. It became K80 in 1935. Inevitably the 1935 scheme had to be modified and its scope broadened as types and sub-types proliferated. Thus the K class, which had been for petrol-engined Tigers, spawned a KA derivative for oil-engined conversions. FM 8165 was fitted with an oil engine in 1949 and was thus renumbered as **KA196**. *(Both: Omnibus Society Midland Branch/Cull Collection)*

DEVELOPMENT OF THE LEYLAND LION

<< Opposite page: The Lion, with four cylinders instead of six, was more economical than the Tiger and was frequently specified for normal stage-carriage use. Leyland's PLSC range gave way to the modernised LT, of which Crosville bought a substantial number. This LT2, No. **376** (**FM 5909**), arrived in 1930 and was photographed when brand new.

Above: The following year's No. **440** (**FM 6420**), another LT2, is seen in service in Llandudno in August 1931.

Below: By 1935 the model designation for the Lion was LT7. This sub-type went into the H class and **H2** (**FM 9000**), with metal-framed Leyland body, is seen when brand new. It was one of the first Crosville buses to enter service with an alpha-numerical fleet number according to the 1935 scheme. *(All: STA/BCVM)*

LEYLAND METAL-FRAMED BODIES

Above: In 1934 a batch of eight TD3 Titans was ordered. Six had Eastern Counties bodywork; the other two were early examples of Leyland's metal-framed product. One of the latter, No. **917 (FM 8150)**, is seen in the Leyland works undergoing the statutory tilt test. Note the sandbags in the background, used to represent passengers when the bus was tilted during the test.

>> *Opposite page:* The following year's Titans were TD4s: six with conventional transmissions and three with torque converters. Leyland bodied all nine, and we illustrate Nos **M18/20 (FM 9054/6)**. The latter was one of the torque-converter machines, which used a form of transmission that cut down on gear-changing but at the cost of increased petrol consumption, and was thus a TD4c. *(All: STA/BCVM)*

COMFORT AND LUXURY

<< *Opposite page:* Number **965** (**FM 8170**) was a 1934 32-seat luxury coach with Duple bodywork dedicated to the Liverpool - London express service. Carrying the green and grey livery, No. 965 was, strangely in view of its duties, another classed as a "bus de luxe" rather than a coach.

Above: Number **742** (**FM 7469**), a 1933 Leyland-bodied TS4, was another so classified. This look at its interior reveals high-backed, well-padded seats, luggage racks and curtains. A bus "de luxe" indeed.

Below: An interesting comparison can be made with 1932's No. **118** (**FM 6873**), a 32-seat Lion LT3 service bus with Leyland bodywork. Plainer seats and no curtains, but luggage racks were provided and the standard of comfort was commendable. *(All: STA/BCVM)*

ACQUIRED TITANS

Above: In 1945 a number of early Leyland Titans were sold by Plymouth Corporation and passed into various Tilling fleets. Crosville took eight, of which **DR 9635** was one. A TD2 with a Mumford 48-seat lowbridge body, it took the Crosville fleet number L79. Its body was rebuilt by Eastern Coach Works in 1946 and a Leyland 8.6-litre oil engine fitted in 1947. This caused a renumbering to **M235**. This photograph was taken in Gwynedd Road, Llandudno, in June 1951. The enormous Tilling destination box could hardly provide a greater contrast to the WID plates. *(GHFA)*

Below: Elderly Titans were still being acquired in 1949, including nine from the Bristol Tramways and Carriage Company Limited. None of them had been new to Bristol. Crosville allocated the fleet number **L115** to the former Ribble vehicle, **CK 4222**, which was a 1930 TD1 with a second-hand Northern Counties 51-seat body taken from a Cardiff Corporation vehicle. Crosville used the bus until 1953. It was standing outside the milk bar in the railway station forecourt at Colwyn Bay in June 1951. These vehicles were purchased to allow as much double-deck operation as possible in the eternal battle against rising costs. *(GHFA)*

EASTERN COACH WORKS REBODYING

In common with several other operators, Crosville undertook a large rebodying programme in the early postwar period, making use of serviceable prewar chassis whose bodywork had worn out. The combination of ECW bodies and prewar bonnet and radiator outlines became quite a feature of many fleets. Crosville's **M25** **(FM 6919)** *(<<< previous page)* was a 1932 Titan TD2 which received a Cov-Rad radiator conversion as well as a standard ECW lowbridge body. **KA192 (FM 7471)** *(above)* was a combination of 1933 Tiger TS4, postwar ECW dual-purpose coachwork and new Cov-Rad radiator, whilst a similar body, to normal service bus standards graced **JA23** **(FM 8993)** *(below)*, a 1935 Lion LT7, which had retained its original radiator. All three photographs were taken in Llandudno, in June 1951. *(All: GHFA)*

POSTWAR LEYLAND TITANS

Above: The combination of Eastern Coach Works bodies and Leyland chassis was not uncommon before 1948. Tilling took a large batch of PD1A Titans with 53-seat lowbridge bodies in 1947 at a time when Bristol could not keep pace with orders. They went to only a few fleets, including Hants & Dorset and 20 to Crosville. **M535** (**GFM 920**) was photographed at West Shore, Llandudno, in June 1951. *(GHFA)*

Below: The most familiar early postwar Leyland was perhaps the PD2 with Leyland's own lowbridge bodywork. Crosville's 1949 examples included eight that had been diverted from Cumberland Motor Services Limited, where the Mageen family, Cumberland's owners, had placed large orders on Leyland before selling out to the BTC. The completed vehicles were all sent to other fleets, thus ensuring that Cumberland became a Bristol fleet. One of them, **M584** (**HRM 704**), again at West Shore in June 1951, shows how the standard Cumberland destination screen, but not the route number boxes, was used by Crosville. *(GHFA)*

AEC REGALS

Perhaps even more of a surprise than the Cumberland Titans, given that Crosville had been such a staunch Leyland fleet that had just become state-owned and henceforth a Bristol customer, was the arrival in 1948/9 of a batch of twelve AEC Regal IIIs with Strachans 35-seat bodywork built to closely resemble the contemporary Eastern Coach Works product. This again was a move in the desperate fight to obtain new vehicles when Bristol and ECW were working to capacity and long delivery delays were being quoted. The AECs started out with the fleet numbers TA1 - 12, but were reclassified SRA901 - 912 in 1958. All twelve were withdrawn in 1961. In this trio of Geoffrey Atkins's June 1951 portraits, we illustrate **TA9 (JFM 579)** at Llandudno *(<< opposite page)*, **TA6 (JFM 576)** *(above)* and **TA7 (JFM 577)** *(below)* at Colwyn Bay. *(GHFA)*

POSTWAR BRISTOLS

Above: State-owned since 1942, Crosville's fleet began in the second half of that decade to take on the familiar look of a green Tilling fleet. One of 1947's many Bristol chassis was **GFM 852**, an AEC-engined L6A with Eastern Coach Works 35-seat bodywork, which entered service with the fleet number KB43. By the time of this August 1959 photograph at Llandudno, it had been rebuilt with a front entrance for driver-only operation and had been renumbered **SLA43**. Separate number blinds had been introduced to relieve the strain on the canopy framing occasioned by the huge - and very long - 48" Tilling one-piece blinds. *(GHFA)*

Below: **JFM 105** was a Bristol K6A (and therefore AEC-engined), which was new in 1949 as MB352. It was **DKA352** in this 1959 view. *(GHFA)*

MORE DIVERTED LEYLANDS

Whereas the diverted Titans *(see page 37)* had been registered by Cumberland Motor Services before being sent to Crosville, the 35 Weymann-bodied PS1/1 Tigers, originally intended for the Midland General Omnibus Company Limited, which were diverted to Crosville in 1950 were unregistered and so took their place in the usual Chester FM series. At various times they carried three different liveries: the all-green service-bus colours, the cream coach livery and a half-and-half cream and green scheme. Originally KA225-59, they were reclassified ETE925-59 in 1958 for express use, and then to STE925-59 in 1962. This latter reversion to service-bus status saw them put back into the green livery. **ETE943 (LFM 318)** *(above)* is shown in cream and green, and **STE929 (LFM 304)** *(below)* had reverted to service-bus use and livery. They were respectively at Conway in August 1959 and at Llandudno. The brightwork on these vehicles instantly revealed the identity of the original intended owner. The simplified main blind had a flip-over plate to cover either the top or centre, thus allowing one display to cover both termini. The flap design was very much akin to that used for many years by East Yorkshire, whence had come Crosville's Chief Engineer, Mr Goodhall. *(GHFA)*

A batch of 18 Duple-bodied 29-seat Bedford OBs arrived in 1950 for tour work. In June of the following year **SL61 (LFM 398)** was at Gwynedd Road, Llandudno. It was withdrawn by Crosville in 1958. *(GHFA)*

Large numbers of Bristols were added to the fleet in 1950, including short and long versions of the single-deck L chassis. The longer LL type came with Gardner (LL5G) or Bristol (LL6B) engines. Among the LL6Bs was **KW187** (**LFM 768**), seen here at Trinity Square, Llandudno, in June 1951. (*GHFA*)

THE BRISTOL LODEKKA

Low bridges carrying railway tracks over roads were always a problem for operators of double-deck buses. It was overcome by the lowbridge design pioneered by Rackham's Leyland Titan in the late 1920s. It was in some ways a compromise solution, because it was necessary to have four-in-a-row seating on the upper deck and a sunken gangway to access them, which protruded into the downstairs headroom. Some designs had three-in-a-row seats and *two* sunken gangways. A quarter of a century later Bristol and Eastern Coach Works produced the Lodekka: a design which retained the lower overall height, but with normal upper-deck seating and no sunken gangway. Crosville was early in the field and in April 1953 **ML661** (**RFM 406**), which was the second production Lodekka, an LD6B (the B signifying a Bristol engine), entered service. It is seen *(above)* working on hire to Midland General at Mount Street, Nottingham the following August. The picture below is of 1954's **RFM 422**, an LD6B with coach seating, luggage space and platform doors, one of eight for use on the Liverpool to Llandudno express service. They originally had twin single-line coach-style destination boxes. ML677 when new, it had been renumbered **DLG677** by the time of this August 1959 Llandudno photograph. *(Both: GHFA)*

DEVELOPMENT OF THE BRISTOL LODEKKA

Above: Nineteen-fifty-three's Lodekka RFM 406, shown on the previous page, had 58 seats, and the coach version 52. **DLB748 (VFM 613)** of 1955, another LD6B, was a 60-seater. It was at Argyle Road, Llandudno, in August 1959. The shortened front mudguards *(compare with RFM 406)* were to overcome engine overheating problems. VFM 613 was withdrawn in 1970. *(GHFA)*

Below: Further variations on the Lodekka theme: 1956's **DLG807 (XFM 218)** was Gardner-engined, and therefore an LD6G. A 60-seater, its platform doors were a later fitment. The shorter grille was an early modification on many Lodekkas. It was at Conway in August 1959. This bus was withdrawn in 1974 and became a Cheshire County Council play bus. *(GHFA)*

UNDERFLOOR-ENGINED SINGLE-DECKERS

Above: Just as the Lodekka came to typify Tilling fleets in the late 1950s and 1960s, so the Bristol LS and later the MW was the usual single-decker. Among Crosville's earliest examples was LS6G **CUG297** (**OFM 669**), delivered in June 1952. The Eastern Coach Works body had 39 coach seats. Fleet numbers are now pressed-metal plates riveted to the body. *(GHFA)*

Below: The LS was an integral chassisless design. The MW which replaced it reverted to a separate chassis. Crosville's **SMG443** (**1222 FM**) was a 41-seat service bus based on the MW6G chassis. It was new in 1963 and was withdrawn in 1979, passing to Silcox, of Pembroke Dock, a well known user of second-hand Bristols. The photograph was taken in June 1970 at Colwyn Bay. Note the unusual fleetname position, necessary because of the provision for an advertisement in the beading above it. *(GHFA)*

UNDERFLOOR-ENGINED BRISTOLS

Above: Many of the Tilling companies used a version of the Eastern Coach Works 45-seat service-bus body shell, fitted with slightly fewer, but more comfortable, seats for "dual-purpose" duties. Crosville's **EMG345 (235 FFM)** was an example. An MW6G new in 1958 as a 41-seater, it was later converted for driver-only operation with 39 seats. It was at Huntingdon Street, Nottingham, in May 1959. *(GHFA)*

Below: The genuine coach body from the ECW factory was usually a 39-seater. Crosville's **CMG516 (7282 FM)** was new in 1964. Withdrawn in 1976, it passed to another independent partial to second-hand Bristol/ECW products, Morris, of Swansea. This is a July 1966 photograph at Llandudno. The livery was cream and black. *(GHFA)*

THE BRISTOL SC

Above: For use on lightly trafficked rural routes, some Tilling operators had a need for a smaller bus than the underfloor-engined Bristol/Eastern Coach Works saloons with 45 seats. The answer was the SC4LK, a front-engined chassis with Gardner four-cylinder engine and a forward-entrance body with 35 seats. Crosville, with more rural routes than most, made good use of the SC. **SSG607 (340 CFM)**, new in 1957, was in Vaughan Street, Llandudno, in August 1959.

Below: The following year's **SSG617 (787 EFM)** was at rest at Gwynedd Road, Llandudno, in June 1961.

>> Opposite page: The SC also appeared as a coach, in this case with 33 seats. **CSG632 (193 KFM)**, a 1959 delivery, was brand new in this August 1959 shot at Trinity Square, Llandudno. These vehicles were without doubt the noisiest and most uncomfortable ever to carry the Bristol/ECW names. A ride on a preserved example will reveal just how dreadful they were. And to use them as coaches ... ! *(All: GHFA)*

49

MORE LODEKKAS

Above: Bristol had allocated the chassis numbers LDX001/2 to the two pre-production Lodekkas. Chassis number LDX003 appeared in the Crosville fleet as **DLG949 (285 HFM)** in 1958. It had the model designation LDS6G and was the first of the flat floor Lodekkas. It was fitted with Cave-Brown-Cave heating, whose heat-exchangers provided cooling for the engine, hence the lack of a radiator grille. This bus was effectively the prototype for the FS series Lodekkas. It was photographed at Llandudno, looking rather battered in NBC ownership, in July 1970. *(GHFA)*

Below: **DLB907 (889 CFM)** was another 1958 delivery, but was a standard LD6B. Both it and the prototype illustrated above had 60 seats and platform doors. An August 1959 photograph at Gwynedd Road. The upper cream band transforms the appearance. Its suppression, as on 285 HFM above, was unfortunate. *(GHFA)*

LODEKKAS BY THE SEASIDE

Above: The idea of special buses, usually with no roofs, or at least with a full-length opening sunshine roof, for use at seaside resorts was an old one. Such vehicles were perhaps less suitable for out-of-season use, and one answer to that was the convertible double-decker. This one was Crosville's **DLB980 (629 HFM)**, dating from 1959. A 60-seater with platform doors, it lasted until 1977. It was at West Shore, Llandudno, in August 1959, running over the old open-top tram route to Old Colwyn.

Below: Another of the same batch, **DLB982 (631 HFM)** was at Conway in the same month. Despite the obviously bright sunshine in that summer month, the roof was firmly on. This was also a 1977 withdrawal from Crosville service. Crosville had pioneered convertible open-top double-deckers in the late 1930s with a batch of Leyland TD5 Titans carrying lowbridge Eastern Coach Works bodywork. *(Both: GHFA)*

This bustling scene at the height of the holiday season was taken in August 1959 in Oxford Road, Llandudno. Several Crosville Lodekkas are visible, led by **DLG1 (611 LFM)**, a Gardner-engined LD6G of 1959. This bus, a 60-seater with platform doors, was converted to permanent open-top specification in 1978, and reregistered ACA 216A in 1984. It was withdrawn in 1985. *(GHFA)*

MORE OPEN-TOP SEASIDE BUSES

Above: **DFG81** (**891 VFM**) was a 1962 Lodekka FSF6G (a front-entrance version of the FS chassis with Gardner six-cylinder engine) with a 60-seat Eastern Coach Works body. It was converted as a seaside open-topper in 1977. After withdrawal it was sold for preservation in 1984. The photograph was taken, from the holiday flat the photographer was renting, at West Parade, Llandudno, in June 1980. *(GHFA)*

Below: Two years earlier the photographer, in June 1978, caught a similar vehicle at Colwyn Bay. **DFG68** (**878 VFM**) had a similar history to that of 891 VFM except for being reregistered ACA 218A in October 1984 and lasting in service until 1985. Note that the former Tilling-style fleetname has now been replaced with the corporate NBC style. *(GHFA)*

Once single-deckers could legally be built to a maximum length of 36 feet, Bristol's response was the rear-engined RE chassis, available with low floorline for bus work, or high for coaching. Eastern Coach Works designed a harmonious body for it, in this case with 47 seats. Crosville's **CRG524 (7285 FM)** was at Argyle Road, Llandudno in July 1966. It was withdrawn in 1980. *(GHFA)*

Further Lodekka coaches, by then on the 30ft-long FLF6B chassis, came in 1962/4. They had 37 seats upstairs but only 18 down, with the rest of the lower deck given over to a large luggage compartment, accessed through the rear emergency door. **DFB149 (AFM 112B)** was new in 1964 and was withdrawn in 1976. (*GHFA*)

DFB200 (EFM 634C) was a standard 70-seat service-bus Lodekka. In September 1972, almost four years into NBC ownership, it was in Oxford Road, Llandudno. The livery was the NBC's corporate leaf-green. *(GHFA)*

COACHES NEW AND OLD

Above: The 39-seat coach on the 30ft-long underfloor-engined MW6G chassis survived for a while after the introduction of the longer RE chassis. **CMG565 (HFM 565D)** arrived in 1966, two years after the introduction of the RE, and lasted 12 years with Crosville. It was photographed in Mostyn Broadway, Llandudno, in July 1966. *(GHFA)*

Below: HFM 565D *(above)* was brand new when photographed; this picture shows an earlier 39-seat coach in its last year with the Company. **CUG323 (OFM 695)** dated from 1953 and was withdrawn in the year of this photograph, 1970. It was an integrally constructed LS6B, seen here in the National Bus Company's "local coach" livery. The bus-style destination indicators were a visually unfortunate graft onto the classic ECW coach profile. *(GHFA)*

BEDFORDS

Above: Bedfords, usually with either Duple or Plaxton bodies, were an everyday sight in scores of fleets in the sixties and seventies - but more often running for independents. The Bedford was relatively uncommon in Tilling fleets though by no means unknown. Crosville's **CVF694 (XFM 694G)** was a VAM70 with Duple 45-seat coachwork. Bedfords were often withdrawn quite quickly in the company fleets, but this one lasted eleven years with Crosville, being withdrawn in 1980. *(GHFA)*

Below: CVT681 (**NFM 681E**), an earlier Bedford acquisition, was a VAM5, also a 45-seater, bodied by Duple (Northern). This 1967 vehicle lasted until 1977. Both photographs were at Llandudno in July 1970. *(GHFA)*

NATIONAL EXPRESS COACHES

Above: The National Bus Company, which came into legal existence on 1st January 1969, decided on an all-white livery, with the NATIONAL fleetname in alternate red and blue letters and a double "N" symbol arranged to resemble an arrow, for its long-distance coaches. In perhaps belated realisation that the old Company names were valuable assets *(W J Crosland Taylor knew all about that 40 years earlier - see page 5)* fleetnames of the originating companies were permitted, but in much smaller lettering. Bristol RE **CRG38 (UFM38F)** was at Nottingham Victoria in July 1974. *(GHFA)*

Below: Many such vehicles were eventually downgraded to "local coach" status and reliveried in a scheme of poppy-red below the windows and white above. **CRG29 (OFM 29E)** was thus turned out when spotted at The Forest, Nottingham, in October 1979. It was working a private hire to Nottingham's famous Goose Fair. *(GHFA)*

THE FLAT-FRONTED RE

The rear-engined Bristol RE was originally a 36ft-long vehicle whether equipped for service-bus or coach bodywork. When a replacement for the underfloor-engined MW was sought, part of the solution was to produce a shorter version of RE which would take 46 service-bus seats. The first few appeared with the RE design's original rounded front but the model soon adopted the later flat front. Crosville's **SRG77/80** (**XFM 77/80G**) were typical RESL6Gs; delivered in 1968, they had uneventful lives and were withdrawn in 1981. These two pictures of them were taken in Mostyn Street, Llandudno, in July 1970. *(Both: GHFA)*

THE FLAT-FRONTED RE

The flat front also appeared on the longer RELL6G model, and Crosville had single-and dual-doorway versions. **SRG137/42 (DFM 137/42H)** were to the the two-door design. They are seen in Conway in July 1970. The space taken up by the centre exit resulted in a reduced seating capacity of 48. These buses were withdrawn in 1981 and 1982. Note that the number blind box is now on the offside, previously always on the nearside going back to single blind days. *(Both: GHFA)*

THE SEDDON PENNINE

Above: The Oldham-based manufacturer, Seddon, in an attempt to attract a share of the annual British bus and coach orders, produced a variety of models. Perhaps the one most likely to appeal to Tilling operators was the rear-engined Pennine RU, which was in direct competition with the Bristol RE. Even so, it was a surprise when Crosville ordered no fewer than 100 for delivery in 1971/2. Fifty were to alleged "dual-purpose" specification, a concept which demanded seating to a standard of comfort closer to the coach than the service bus. It was felt in some quarters that these Seddons did not justify that expectation. **EPG748 (OFM748K)** was at Llandudno in September 1972. *(GHFA)*

Below: **SPG797 (OFM 797K)** was one of the other 50 Pennine RUs, which were dual-doorway 45-seat service buses. A number were later converted to single-door layout. The bus was at West Shore, Llandudno, also in September 1972. Expensive to maintain and unreliable, the Seddons were heartily disliked by maintenance staff and drivers; bad buy that they were, they nevertheless survived for ten years. Upon withdrawal, the Gardner engines from 98 of them were fitted to Leyland Nationals. *(GHFA)*

THE RETURN OF LEYLAND

Above: For some years, following the absorption of Crosville into the state-owned network, Leyland chassis were conspicuous by their absence in Crosville's annual orders. Following the closure of Bristol once British Leyland had got its hands on it, the Lancashire *marque* again appeared in the fleet. **CLL318 (RMA 318P)**, a Leopard PSUC3C/4R, with Plaxton (Leyland had also closed down Eastern Coach Works) 49-seat coachwork, was delivered in July 1976. It was withdrawn in 1987. In this sunlit June 1978 view, it was at Mostyn Broadway, Llandudno. *(GHFA)*

Below: Similar vehicle **RMA 314P** is seen two years later after demotion to "local coach" livery and repainting in the appropriate NBC livery for such duties. Its fleet number had been changed to **ELL314** from the original CLL314 at the time of the demotion. The photograph was taken in Llandudno in June 1980. *(GHFA)*

INTO THE NBC ERA

Above: Just as the Bristol RE took over from the MW, the double-deck FLF Lodekka was replaced by the rear-engined VR. Bristol was rather late into the rear-engined double-decker field, and even then there were difficulties: Crosville, for instance, found that for use on city work, brake linings had to be changed almost weekly. Such problems were overcome, and the VR can now be seen as perhaps the best of the first generation of such designs. Crosville's **DVL332 (UMB 332R)** was a VRT/SL3/501 (which meant that it had a Leyland engine) with 74-seat Eastern Coach Works bodywork. In November 1988 it was destroyed by fire at Rock Ferry depot. *(GHFA)*

Below: The Leyland National was controversial at and for some time after its launch. Leyland's initial insistence on offering the operator only what it wished to manufacture did not help (the refusal, for example, to offer a Gardner-engined version). With hindsight, however, it can be appreciated that it was a sound design which gave good value for money once the initial snags had been ironed out. This one, **SNL362 (EMB 362S)**, was new to Crosville in June 1978 as a 49-seater. It was fitted with a Gardner engine from a Crosville Seddon in October 1988 and reclassified SNG362. This view of it in Llandudno dates from June 1984. *(GHFA)*